QUIZ # 28755
BL 4.3
AR Pts 0.5

W9-BZU-871

FAMILIES AROUND THE WORLD

A family from
BOSNIA

Julia Waterlow

RSVP

RAINTREE
STECK-VAUGHN
PUBLISHERS
The Steck-Vaughn Company

Austin, Texas

FAMILIES AROUND THE WORLD

A family from **BOSNIA**

A family from **BRAZIL**

A family from **CHINA**

A family from **ETHIOPIA**

A family from **GERMANY**

A family from **GUATEMALA**

A family from **IRAQ**

A family from **JAPAN**

A family from **SOUTH AFRICA**

A family from **VIETNAM**

Cover: The Bucalovic family outside their apartment with all their possessions
Title page: The Bucalovic family on their balcony
Contents page: People waiting in line for water in Sarajevo

Picture Acknowledgments: All the photographs in this book were taken by Alexandra Boulat. The photographs were supplied by Material World/ Impact Photos, and were first published by Sierra Club Books in 1994. © Copyright Alexandra Boulat/Material World.

© Copyright 1998, text, Steck-Vaughn Company

All rights reserved. No part of this book may be reproduced or utilized in any form or by any means, electronic or mechanical, including photocopying, recording, or by any information storage and retrieval system, without permission in writing from the Publisher. Inquiries should be addressed to: Copyright Permissions, Steck-Vaughn Company, P.O. Box 26015, Austin, TX 78755.

Published by Raintree Steck-Vaughn Publishers, an imprint of Steck-Vaughn Company

Library of Congress Cataloging-in-Publication Data
Waterlow, Julia.
A family from Bosnia / Julia Waterlow.
p. cm.—(Families around the world)
Includes bibliographical references and index.
Summary: Traces the daily life of a family in Sarajevo from the time the city came under siege in November 1992 until a peace agreement was enforced and elections held in 1996.
ISBN 0-8172-4901-X
1. Sarajevo (Bosnia and Herzegovina)—History—Siege, 1992-1996—Juvenile literature.
[1.Sarajevo (Bosnia and Herzegovina)—History—Siege, 1992-1996.]
I. Title. II. Series: Families around the world.
DR1313.32.S27W38   1998
949.703—dc21   96-54904

Printed in Italy. Bound in the United States.
1 2 3 4 5 6 7 8 9 0 02 01 00 99 98

Contents

Introduction 4

Meet the Family 6

A Home in Sarajevo 8

Food and Cooking 14

Working Together 18

School and Play 24

Time to Relax 26

Hope for Peace 28

Pronunciation Guide 30

Glossary 31

Books to Read 31

Index 32

◈ Introduction

Bosnia was once part of a much bigger country called Yugoslavia.

REPUBLIC OF BOSNIA-HERZEGOVINA

Capital city:	Sarajevo
Size:	19,741 sq. mi. (51,130 sq. km.)
Number of people:	3,201,823
Main Language:	Serbo-Croatian (official)
People:	Bosnian Muslims 44%, Serbs 31%, Croats 17%
Religions:	Muslim, Christian (The Serbs belong to the Eastern Orthodox Church, and the Croats are Catholic.)
Currency:	New Yugoslavian Dinar

THE BUCALOVIC FAMILY

Size of household:	5 people
Size of home:	645 sq. ft. (60 sq. m.)
Workweek:	0 hours (Adults are paid for civilian labor.)
Most valued possessions:	Lokman: Medical book, radio; Nafja: Electric lamp
Family income:	$25 per month (army pay)

The Bucalovic family is an average Bosnian family. The Bucalovics have put everything that they own outside their home so that this photograph could be taken.

Meet the Family

1 Arina, mother, 26
2 Nedzad, father, 23
3 Nadja, daughter, 2

4 Lokman, grandfather, 67
5 Nafja, grandmother, 65

A COUNTRY OF CHANGE

Bosnia was once part of a country called Yugoslavia. Three main groups of people—Muslims, Croats, and Serbs—live there. When Bosnia became an independent country, these groups started fighting each other. The Serbs either killed or forced many Muslims to leave their homes.

On a dark night in November 1992, the Serb army attacked the Muslim town where the Bucalovic family lived. Nedzad, Arina, and Nadja fled. After six hours of walking, they arrived at Arina's parents' home in the city of Sarajevo. All they had with them were the clothes they wore. They all went to live in Arina's parents' third-floor apartment.

"Life in Sarajevo is often boring but then suddenly very scary."—*Arina*

A Home in Sarajevo

Arina's parents' apartment, where the Bucalovic family lives. It has four small rooms and views of the hills around the city.

UNDER ATTACK!

In 1993, Sarajevo was surrounded and under attack from the Serbs. There was often bombing and shooting, and the buildings were hit by shells. The streets were not safe, so Bosnians used to spend a lot of time inside.

The Safest Room

The family's apartment has a living room that faces out on to the main street. The family didn't use this room much during the war because it was on the side most likely to be hit by shells and bullets. Lokman built a barricade across the room so the bullets couldn't get through.

Most of the time, the family stayed in the kitchen at the back of the apartment. Although it was rather dark, they felt safer there. Lokman slept on the sofa in the living room, with Nedzad and Arina on a mattress on the floor beside him.

This room used to be Nafja's and Lokman's bedroom. During the war it became a place where the family stored things.

Waiting for Light

After the war started, electricity and water only came on every now and then. So Nafja always kept her electric lamp switched on. The lamp was very important to her because when it came on, she knew the electricity was working.

Nadja sometimes helped her mother by filling the bathtub. This gave the family enough water for a few days.

"When the water was working, we had to fill the bath quickly. We never knew when it would stop working again."—*Arina*

Nafja tried to keep warm and read although there was often no electricity.

Making Do

It can get very cold in the winter in Sarajevo. After the gas was cut off, the Bucalovics' only heat came from a stove in the kitchen. They could not always get wood for the stove, so Lokman soaked paper and cardboard in water and rolled them into hard balls. He left the paper balls to dry out on the balcony. He then burned these balls of paper in the stove.

Lokman used paper to make balls to burn in the stove.

▲ Nadja joins other people in the basement. This was the safest place to be when there was a lot of bombing.

When the bombing was bad, the Bucalovics and other families in the building would stay in the basement. Nadja's parents spent so much time in the cellar that they hated it. Arina and Nedzad preferred to risk staying in the apartment. But they still sent Nadja down.

Food and Cooking

HIGH PRICES

Because Sarajevo was under attack and surrounded by Serb forces, it was difficult for food to reach the city. Most stores were closed, and there was not much food in the street markets. It was also very expensive—just one carrot cost $3 and two pounds of meat $32— more than a month's income.

Instead of a gas range, the Bucalovics cooked on a wood-burning stove.

The family usually started the day with tea, cheese, and bread. The bakery did not always have bread, so often Arina or Nafja baked it at home. Nadja likes drinking milk, but the Bucalovics were not able buy fresh milk for more than a year.

An Evening Meal

Nedzad enjoys a good meal after coming home late.

One of the family's favorite dishes is tomato and onion salad. The Bucalovics would have this with their main meal in the evening when they could find good food in the market. Arina or Nafja often cooked the family a main dish made of rice, canned meat, and potatoes.

Fresh Food

With the war going on, any kind of fresh food, such as vegetables, fruit, or meat, was hard to find. The Bucalovics were given extra food by the United Nations every month. The United Nations gave them cans of meat and fish, flour, beans, and sugar.

Arina walks through the market, looking for some fresh food.

Arina would go to the market to look for
potatoes and fruit. Sometimes she came home
with nothing because the food was too
expensive or not good. Often the vegetables
were too old and dried up.

"I used to grow roses, but
you can't eat them. So I
started growing tomatoes
instead."—*Lokman*

Working Together

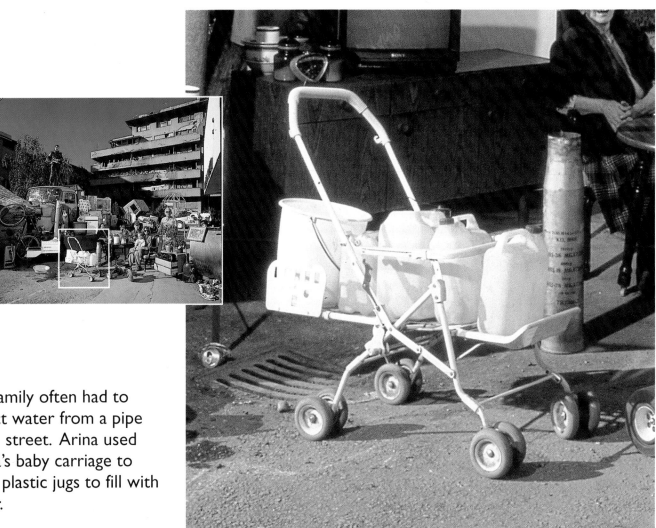

The family often had to collect water from a pipe in the street. Arina used Nadja's baby carriage to carry plastic jugs to fill with water.

WARTIME JOBS

Everyone in Bosnia was caught up in the war, and few people had normal jobs. Some were fighting and some were refugees. Others, such as doctors, helped in hospitals looking after the people who had been wounded.

Surviving

Lokman and Nafja helped around the house. Lokman liked gardening on the balcony when it was quiet. This was risky because he could have been shot. Only Arina and Nedzad went out into the streets to get supplies.

In Sarajevo Arina spent most of her time finding the basic things the family needed to survive. One of her jobs was to go and collect water when there was none in the apartment. She used to take lots of plastic jugs and load them into Nadja's baby carriage. She then walked to a public faucet to fill them. When she got home, Arina had to carry them all up to the apartment.

Arina lines up in the street for water.

At War

For eight days at a time, Nedzad used to leave home to join the Bosnian army. The army was fighting the Serbs. He had to make the dangerous journey on foot into the mountains around Sarajevo.

Nedzad in his Bosnian army uniform

Nedzad was a hairdresser before the war. During the war he liked to keep in practice by doing Nafja's and Arina's hair. Both women liked to look as good as possible, even though they hardly ever went out. Nedzad did his best, even though he did not have shampoo or a blow-dryer.

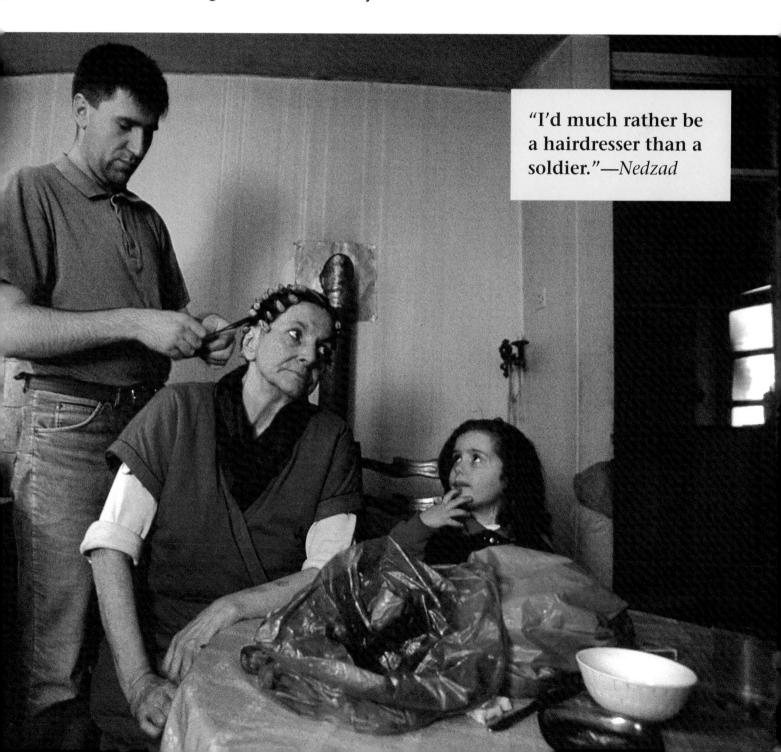

"I'd much rather be a hairdresser than a soldier."—*Nedzad*

Danger Outside

When Nedzad came back home from fighting, he used to help Arina get food and wood. Often they couldn't go out because the city was being bombed by the Serbs. But when it was quiet, Nedjad and Arina set off to find supplies. Even then, shells or bullets could suddenly hit buildings or people in the streets. Nedzad and Arina had to move very carefully.

Nedzad fills his backpack with wood. He bought the wood from a friend.

Arina stores the wood that Nedzad bought on the balcony.

School and Play

EDUCATION

Where there was fighting, schools in Bosnia were closed. Many of the buildings were destroyed. Before the war, Bosnians were well educated—88 percent of women and 97 percent of men could read and write.

During the war, Nadja's parents didn't allow her to ride her bike out on the streets.

Every morning during the war, the radio told whether the schools would be open. Many had been bombed or else they were full of refugees. Sometimes it was too dangerous for the children to go to school. When a school was open, children of all ages often had to crowd into one room.

"In this house there are two dangers: the war and little Nadja!"
—*Lokman*

Nadja used to play out on the balcony with the boy next door. They played soldiers with his plastic machine gun.

Playing at Home

Nadja was too young to go to school during the war. Most of her time was spent in the apartment. Her parents did not dare let her go outside in case she got shot. Instead, Nadja played with other children inside or sometimes out on the balcony.

Time to Relax

This radio was important to the Bucalovics. It helped them keep in touch with the war news.

DANGER

Before the war, many people in Bosnia used to take vacations at the seashore or travel to other nearby countries. During the war, most people couldn't even leave their towns or homes because of the dangers.

The Bucalovics had a car before fighting broke out and used to go on family outings. During the war all their spare time was spent inside. Lokman liked to listen to the radio or read his favorite book.

Arina loves shopping, clothes, and makeup. When she came to Sarajevo all she had were blue jeans, a sweater, a warm coat, and a pair of shoes. A friend gave her some other clothes to wear. But Arina misses being able to go shopping and to buy new clothes.

When it was quiet in the evening, Lokman used to lie down or read by candlelight.

Hope for Peace

Life is getting better for the Bucalovic family. The shooting in Sarajevo has stopped, and supplies of food are getting through. Arina and Nedzad want to leave Sarajevo and to start a new life, with a modern house and furniture. Most of all, they want Bosnia to stay peaceful.

Nedzad prays at the grave of a friend of his who died in the war.

"Bosnia will never be the same."—*Nedzad*

THE WAR IS OVER

A peace agreement has now been signed among the Muslims, Serbs, and Croats, and Bosnia has held elections. Although the war has stopped, many Bosnians are sad and bitter because they have lost their families and homes.

Nedzad and Nadja are happy that the war seems to be over.

Pronunciation Guide

Arina	Ah-**ree**-nah
Bosnia	Boz-nee-ah
Bucalovic	Boo-ka-**loh**-vitch
Herzegovina	Hairt-zeh-goh-vee-nah
Lokman	**Lock**-mun
Nedzad	**Ned**-zhad
Nadja	**Nah**-dee-ah
Nafja	**Nah**-fee-ah
Sarajevo	sah-rah-**yay**-voh
Yugoslavia	you-goh-**slahv**-ee-ah

Glossary

Barricade A barrier to keep harmful objects from getting through.

Elections When people vote to choose their new leaders.

Grave A place where a dead person is buried.

Independent country A country that rules itself and is not controlled by another.

Muslims People who follow the Islamic religion.

Peace agreement An agreement made by different sides in a war to stop fighting.

Refugees People who have had to leave their homes because of war or other troubles and have nowhere to go.

Shells Exploding bombs that are fired from big guns.

United Nations An organization made up of countries around the world. The United Nations works to bring peace and a better life for everyone.

Books to Read

Ganeri, Anita. *I Remember Bosnia*. Why We Left. Austin, TX: Raintree Steck-Vaughn, 1994.

McLeish, Ewan. *Europe*. Continents. Austin, TX: Raintree Steck-Vaughn, 1997.

Riccioti, Edward R. *War in Yugoslavia: The Breakup of a Nation*. Headliners. Brookfield, CT: Millbrook Press, 1993.

Rody, Martyn. *The Breakup of Yugoslavia*. Conflicts. Morristown, NJ: Silver Burdett Press, 1994.

Index

army 7, 20

bombing 8, 13, 22, 24

clothes 27
Croats 4, 6, 29

elections 29
electricity 10, 11

food 14–17, 29

heating 12
hospitals 18
housing 8–9

jobs 18, 19, 21

language
  Serbo-Croatian 4

markets 14, 16, 17

peace 28–29

radio 24, 26
refugees 18, 24

schools 24
Serbs 4, 6, 7, 8, 14, 20,
  22, 29, 30
shopping 14, 27
shelter 13

United Nations 16

vacations 26

water 10, 19
wood 12, 22, 23

Yugoslavia (former)
  4, 6

© Copyright 1997 Wayland (Publishers) Ltd.